POSITIVE AFFIRMATION - FEAR NO MORE

Memoir

Some Suggestions to Reverse Type 2 Diabetes

Anne Marie Herman

authorHOUSE®

AuthorHouse™
1663 Liberty Drive
Bloomington, IN 47403
www.authorhouse.com
Phone: 1 (800) 839-8640

Published by AuthorHouse 01/09/2020

ISBN: 978-1-7283-4124-8 (sc)
ISBN: 978-1-7283-4125-5 (hc)
ISBN: 978-1-7283-4123-1 (e)

Print information available on the last page.

CONTENTS

Coming to The United States Challenge Continues

My husband and I got married in Castries, St. Lucia in 1968. Prior to that, we were engaged for eight years and counting. The engagement lasted long because my husband left the police force in St. Lucia, the West Indies, and went to the U.S. Virgin Islands to work. We kept the relationship alive by writing to each other every week. At some point, we broke up while absence makes the heart grow stronger, and got back together again. This became a long-distance relationship on the opposite coasts of America.

After we became a married couple, we got two British passports in St. Lucia. The day after, we traveled to Barbados, West Indies to obtain permanent documents to enter into the United States of America legally. We obtained a permanent visa in Barbados, so that I could join him at Fort Carson, Colorado Springs later. It took at least two days to meet with the officials at the American Consulate in Barbados. We got a chest X-Rays and physical examination for medical records, as this was a legal and important requirement to enter into U.S territories. The officials provided an envelope with my X-Ray inside so that when I was ready to enter the U.S, I would have sufficient documents to go through customs. The officials at the customs kept my visa, in Puerto Rico, as this was the first port of entry, and I was able to continue to join my husband where he was stationed in the U.S Army.

Three months later, I hopped a plane and traveled to Puerto Rico, then to New York, and Colorado Springs. There was a problem in Puerto Rico. It was difficult at the airport because the majority of the check-in staff spoke Spanish and they did not use the English language. They took me to someone who spoke English, and that's when I discovered the plane had already left. Therefore, I missed my connection, and the plane left without me, oh well. Over the years, the airport procedures have changed. Luckily for me that day, the same plane I missed on the way to New York crashed and everyone on board died. I was surprised to hear about the tragedy, and did not know my luggage was taken away on that plane. For a moment I wondered what was I going to do. Had to take a different plane number to New York. When I heard about the story, I thought God was looking out for me. When I reached in Colorado Springs, I had no luggage except what I was wearing. My husband went berserk not knowing what to say. His wife coming to join him and had no other clothes to wear. Next day, it was snowing in Colorado Springs. Imagine that I came from a warm country with 84 degrees temperature year-round.

Finally, I realized I had no coat, no sweater, but needed to shop at Sears Roebuck to purchase some more clothes. It seems it did not matter after my arrival in Colorado Springs, since we were in the arms of each other. We had to catch the bus too. When I saw little flakes coming down, I asked my husband, what's that. He told me it was snowing, it would melt, but the flakes do not stay on the ground too long. Right after we purchased some more clothes, the airline delivered my luggage two weeks later.

When we left Barbados, we returned to St. Lucia after obtaining our legal papers. My husband stayed in St. Lucia for a week and went back to Colorado Springs as he was on a 30-day vacation.

After arriving in Colorado Springs, I started looking for a job. Then it became apparent to me that I was not qualified for certain classifications. Since I had just entered the country, the jobs I really wanted would not be given to me. I got a Social Security number, but jobs were not readily available because I was emigrated from a foreign country, and I was new in the state. Then I finally started to work at the Broadmoor Hotel as a machine operator. I really did not want to make this a career, because most of the people at the job site spoke no English, so I had to search for work elsewhere and went to the Urban League. They advised me since I was a private school teacher before, it would be wiser to get a teaching certificate or go take some college courses. I decided to attend the El Paso Community College in a Work Study Program. The staff at EPCC were puzzled that I was keeping up with my studies, despite the fact that I had two children and still got good grades.

I finished an Associate in Science degree and still did not know what I was going to do with myself.

While I was employed at the El Paso Community College during the summer, I applied for citizenship. That ceremony was held in Denver Colorado, which was about 70 miles from Colorado Springs. The staff from the Urban League accompanied us to Denver. On the way to Denver, the staff from the Urban League asked me several questions about citizenship to see whether I remembered the answers I had studied and practiced.

I was asked 13 questions by the examiner, but when I met with the other contestants, they indicated 8 questions were asked. One of the questions was a puzzle for me, and I was hesitant to answer the question. I noticed something on the wall in that office, and I summarized that to form an answer for one of the citizenship questions. Then the examiner told me I was done. I was not sure whether that question was planted there to see if I could read English, but it sure helped me to answer the question needed to pass the citizen test.

I worked for the Operation and Maintenance Service, a Project Headquarters for the Air Force in Purchasing. This was a temporary job from Manpower Employment Agency, but OMS decided to keep everyone permanent and full time. That was an excellent job, but they had very strict rules as they made purchases for government agency contracts. I proofed Purchasing Agents orders, and when I found any miscalculation errors, I took the work back to the agent. While I was employed at OMS, the swear-in ceremony was held in Denver. The staff at OMS bought me a cake and invited everyone from the plant to come and wish me congratulations before leaving for Denver. They had the American flags hanging at the office and balloons. They asked me how did I feel now as I was about to become a citizen. I was afraid for a while thinking if war breaks, I would have no place to hide.

Right after my husband resigned from the Army, he joined the Colorado Springs Police Department as a civilian. He worked nights and I was at home with the two kids. Then my husband lost his job in the police force shortly afterwards, and we went back to St. Lucia for six months. We stayed at my mother's residence and also my husband's mother's home just visiting and catching up on what was happening while we were away. New roads were built in St. Lucia and where my mother-in-law stayed the government took some of the space to extend the highway.

After I terminated the job at Operation and Maintenance Service, the supervisor contacted the school (EPCC) to search for a replacement person with my caliber and knowledge. They were not lucky to find another student like me to hire. We had two children while I was going to school. Later, we moved to Wisconsin, and was hired at the Rayovac Corporation after one try and stayed there for 10 years doing transcription and forecast work and other duties. Today, I am retired and have written a cookbook that was published in 2018.

In 1973-74, my family left Madison to travel to St. Lucia via Miami, Florida. When we arrived in Miami, we discovered there was bad weather in St. Lucia and no planes could land there, as the airport was closed. The airline never notified us that there was inclement weather problem, and the travel plans were in vain. We stayed at the airport overnight and we returned back to Madison the next day.

Family Issues/Pass Over in Class

I attended the Babonneau primary school. At that school, a long time ago, I was passed over in a class and held back. The reason being, a student copied on me during an exam, and the principal thought I copied on her. I could not understand the whole thing. This student was very pretty and attractive with long hair, but she was not bright at all. The principal sent her to the next level class and left me in the same class. When the other teacher asked me why was I in that class, I told him that there was an error made by the principal. The teacher Patterson Touissant asked me to do the problems on the board for a higher class and he also called out spelling words fast for me to write quickly. I passed both the mental arithmetic and other subjects. The teacher transferred me to two classes higher than where the principal left me.

I studied at the Kenley's College while taking evening classes in English, math, geography. I also taught English, math, recreation. I went to the Extra Mural school in St. Lucia. There was a problem at the College as some of the student's parents were not paying their tuition on a timely manner. Therefore, the principal had a problem paying his teachers on a timely basis. Sometimes I had to go to the bank many times before I could cash my check. This was a private school where money had to be deposited first before the teachers could get paid. When the school decided to travel to another village, I did not participate, instead I went to a wholesale store to look for a job, and was hired on the spot. At the Extra Mural school, I wrote essays about the dictionary. I was famous playing school with some of the students that went to the Kenley's College. That's when we discovered the spelling of the state Mississippi while setting up a filing system. We learned the difference between diminish and relinquish.

School Master Leaves Desk to Catch Late Students

Many years ago, while attending the Babonneau primary school in St. Lucia, the principal (school master) would leave his desk on mornings and walked up the road to see which student arrived at school late. If we were caught, he would ask that we stay outside and wait till he returns. He would ask us to form a line and come to him to say why we were coming in late. Then he took his whip and strike us on the back. Today, teachers do not have that kind of flexibility in the school system, or taking chances to do such a thing so that a parent can sue the school.

Life has changed for school children, and more can be done to prevent this kind of behavior. The principal (school master) changed his behavior after the children's parents complained. Instead of beating the children, he would make them write sentences many times on a piece of paper. During those years, we had neither school buses nor transportation, but walked to school. The only transportation for school was for colleges and not primary schools.

When our children started going to elementary school, we made sure they arrived on time. If they missed the school bus, one of us would take them to school until they were able to drive themselves.

At the Kenley's college, the principal used his belt or his hand to whoop the students for not doing homework or school work.

I played school with my cousins practicing Pitman Shorthand. If I had to change books writing shorthand, I practiced the brief forms prior to school reopening, therefore, I was always on top of my class.

I also went to typing school to learn typing on a manual typewriter. The keys were so far apart. Today, it is much better to have a keyboard. I was tested at the Miss Benjamin Typing School but the test was graded in London, England and got an Intermediate score. At that time, England was controlling St. Lucia and was the mother country.

At Babonneau primary school, I was a Girl Scout and marched to church on Sunday mornings in my scout uniform. I left scouting as a Cadet Ranger. I learned a lot about the Morris Codes. I was also involved in the church choir singing the songs in mostly Latin language which I missed dearly today. In school we prayed at lunch time, we said grace before meals. "Bless us oh Lord and these thy gifts which we are going to receive from thy bounty through Christ our Lord amen". As a matter of fact, we practiced music as the scouts were actually the choir for the church.

While I was teaching at the Kenley's College, I fell in love with my boyfriend when I was 16. At that time, I was living at my oldest brother's house doing housework. I also cooked, sewed nearly all my clothes that I wanted to wear the same day without a pattern by measuring my body. My brother Jerome was a taxi driver in St. Lucia after he came from London, England for six years. He wore white long sleeve shirts driving tourist to hotels and surrounding areas. I washed and ironed all those white shirts by hand.

When I met my boyfriend, who has been my husband for many years now, he was working as a mechanic. Each morning I would go down the Chisel Street, and he would watch me. If he noticed another mechanic watching me or tried to say hello to me, he would tell them this one is mine and to leave her alone. Today, we have two grown children and two grandchildren with one going to the university, and the other goes to a technical college.

While my boyfriend was still in the police force, I would sneak out from school and joined him at his mother's house. His mother always traveled to other islands and returned when she was done with her shopping for merchandise to sell in her store. Sometimes we would drink his mother's wine or white grape juice. At times we would go to the beach nearby. On holidays, I would leave town and go dancing at the primary school. My boyfriend never wanted to go out dancing as he was claiming to be a Seven Day Adventist. Sometimes my oldest brother would be looking for me and could not find me. He would eventually visit my mother-in-law's house asking for me and she would say she had not seen me while I was there hiding inside her home.

After my boyfriend left the police force, he went to the Virgin Islands. We kept writing to each other. When I left St. Lucia, the letters were in a box not knowing when I would return to the house. My boyfriend would say "you always have homework" to do. My oldest brother created trouble for us saying he would leave you alone and go after other girls. It was a constant battle between my brothers, as I was the only sister in St. Lucia and was always trying to chase the guys away from me. During that time, I did lots of walking and had a voluptuous shape that my boyfriend was boasting about. In the Virgin Islands, he would tell the shops/merchants that he had a girlfriend with a size of 24 waist X34 bust and X36 hips.

My third oldest brother Etienne was a tailor, sewed clothes for his customers, and planted and sold bananas once or twice a week. He also carried merchandise for businesses in St. Lucia with his truck. For a while doctors discovered he had diabetes and had to give him insulin. He was not using the medication prescribed, but that also expired. He kept on getting more uncapable of handling himself. He got somewhat desperate and asked his son to see whether he could get a refill. By then, the doctor would not refill any of his prescriptions, unless he would revisit the clinic. He became sick and died from prostate cancer, and seizures. When I contacted my brother before he passed, he indicated that he had medicine to take and it was difficult to swallow the medication prescribed. I asked him to use a bigger glass of water. He answered that he had more than one pill to take, will he have to drink a large glass for each pill? I told him to take small sips of water. The doctors charged $500 for each visit. When I called again to see how he was doing, he was at the hospital and that's where he died. The other problem was that my brother switched to a different religion and thought god would handle him better in heaven and that he would have nothing to worry about.

My second oldest brother, Robert, was having financial difficulties and informed me about the situation. My oldest brother Jerome indicated that Robert was not having financial problems, and that he was building a house for a woman and that was draining his income. He asked me if I wanted to buy my grand-father's old house in Castries, as the grand-father had left the house for him in case he died. I replied sure; I will purchase it from you. I sent some money to my brother. He was in the process of creating a deed for me. We kept on corresponding to each other and he died and did nothing about it. My sister took over and got the deed.

Robert was a pretty good as a taxi driver and he frequently came to pick me up from work if it was raining. If the sun was very hot, he would advise me to use an umbrella. Sometimes when

Robert was going home late in the night if he saw an ice cream truck on the road, he would stop to buy ice cream for his little sister in the night and I would eat it then. At that time, we did not have a refrigerator.

When myself and my family visited St. Lucia, Robert always purchased fish by the market and brought it to my mother-in-law's house and also brought Cadbury chocolates to my children. Each time they saw him coming, they were looking for candy. He was a remarkable brother, and I miss him tremendously as I did not go to his funeral. I was afraid to go there alone as it was an emergency. In St. Lucia, they usually bury you the next day after your death.

Robert's lawyer tried for me to purchase his home while the family was settling his properties, but I thought it would be difficult because when he was building his last house, I went to the place to help cleaning any residue paint left on the windows and the floors.

Robert was my immediate contact for any issues in St. Lucia. Anything I needed from St. Lucia, I called Robert. Even my broken gold earrings I sent to him to get fixed at a local jeweler. By the time I went to St. Lucia after his death, the cemetery plot was already gone.

All of us overseas depended on Robert to solve issues, but now he is gone and things are not like it was before. I learned a lot by taking care of my brothers, but God had a better plan and place for them in heaven.

My youngest brother, Reginald called me from St. Lucia and said he was coming to Madison so come and pick him up at the airport. I got all excited and went to the Dane County airport to pick him up. My brother was not there. I came back to the house and called Robert in St. Lucia about Reginald not coming up. Robert indicated he was not telling the truth, he lied to me and was somewhat half drunk. When I told Robert about the story he got pretty upset because that was not the right thing to do. Instead that night my sister called to say Robert died from a heart attack. Reginald also died from cancer after Robert's death. He too went to heaven.

My brother Jerome died from a heart attack while he was in the hospital waiting to be treated in the emergency room area. First, another driver saw him in his vehicle on the side of the road in St. Lucia, and realized that he needed help and called 911. At the hospital they make you wait for a long time sometimes and with all the exhaustion from driving tourist, my brother died.

FAMILY ISSUES

The author's father died from Malaria at age 35. The reason for his death has been a mystery. He either ate something or was bitten by a snake as he had a property that had rattle snakes. I never saw a picture of him alive. I presume mother did not have a camera at that time. I was only 18 months old and the rest of the family were very young so details are somewhat sketchy.

It was different at my mother's house as we had to carry water from an oasis with a bucket every day unless there was heavy rain. We also had to go to a river to wash clothes. If it rained, we could not wash clothes as the water would be muddy. We also collected water in drums or septic tanks next to the house. The kitchen was a little house by itself.

There were lots of mango trees that provided juicy mangoes. There were plenty of coconut trees and we drank coconut water. Some of the coconuts would turn into copra when the water inside the coconut dried out. My mom sold coconuts, breadfruits, yams, limes, guavas, tannia, avocados, dasheen and farina by the vegetable market.

My mother Rita died in 1976 from heart failure. She also had kidney problems, as her knees were always swollen. We were not sure how old she was when she died as we could not locate her birth certificate. She looked like she was in her 60's in her pictures.

My mother Rita sold lemonade by a church in St. Lucia. In those days, we called lemonade "squash" because we had to squeeze the juice from limes to make squash. The process was a challenge because those days we did not have a refrigerator at home. We purchased ice from an "ice factory" which was located in the middle of the town Castries the capital for St. Lucia.

On Saturdays, we purchased a block of ice and picked it up later in the day on the way home in the countryside. The ice factory coated sawdust over the ice. The ice block measured 18" X 18". A commuter bus assisted in the process by picking up the ice at the factory. Close to the church, there was a house where this ice was kept overnight. We had to put sawdust over the bag of ice to prevent it from melting. On Sunday morning, we picked up the ice and placed it where it would be used to make squash and sold to churchgoers. Two people had to carry the ice in a Burlap bag. An ice pick was used to break the ice.

Mom made saltfish cakes by the church and sold to the churchgoers. We sold saltfish cakes by dance halls and society halls where society friends would attend meetings or at polling places.

We made saltfish cakes at home as appetizers and to entertain groups of people coming from a long distance from where we lived.

During Christmas time, lots of people came to the home celebrating with made-up songs, and played drums. We baked sourdough bread and stewed mutton for the groups. They drank white rum and shoot the breeze about life, love, and hearsay and sometimes my mom would start to cry as her second husband Reggie would not come to the house when all those people were around.

My grandfather, Bertrand was the real father we lost at the age of 102 years old. We depended on him. Laying on his death bed, he did not look like he was dead. He used to have a nose bleed. I cried and rolled on the floor screaming, knowing that I would not see him again. He was the first family I evidenced being dead at that time. He was buried at Gros Islet in St. Lucia. I was only 15 years old. He was like a "happy go lucky" type of person. He liked white rum, dancing at the society halls, and had a jovial and friendly attitude. His merry and playful caliber kept him living for a long time. He married my grandmother Affie when he was young. My grandfather could not write his own name in St. Lucia, but he knew what he had to do to take care of his son's children. When Affie died, she had no hair left on her head. Affie died before my grandfather and he got married again.

At home, after school, I stopped at my grandfather's house. He always had cooked food on the fire for if in case I stopped by. He also liked to ride horses and the donkey, he raised lots of chickens. You can hear the cock crows early in the morning at my grandfather's house. He planted lots of gardens near his home and lots of coconuts, avocados, yams, mangoes of all kinds, breadfruits and to name a few. After my grandfather died, my uncle, Feddy took over and made our lives miserable with his restrictions as my grandfather eliminated him from his will.

My grandmother Affie was born in Dominica, West Indies. Affie married my grandfather, Bertrand and they had two sons, Gerald my father and Feddy my uncle. My sister Helena checked at the registry in St. Lucia to find out whether there was anything recorded on my grandmother. Up to this day, we have not located Affie's birth certificate or supported documentation to know more about her family. Usually, when people from other islands move to St. Lucia, they were either in some kind of trouble or dispute and came to find a place to hide. My sister was scared of my grandmother, as she was pretty strict. Therefore, when my mother was away from home, my sister would stay at the neighbor's home instead visiting our grandmother Affie.

My uncle Feddy left St. Lucia and went to British Guiana and from there he went to Cuba. He came back from Cuba with nothing but a cutlass. He cut quite a number of mango trees down from properties my grandfather left for us. He was upset as he discovered that my grandfather eliminated him from his will. Feddy played tricks on us claiming that he was deaf or had hearing impaired problems; and that he could only hear some of the families he cared for. He behaved like a bad guy and destroyed quite a bit of crops around all the houses in the neighborhood which was family land.

My sister had her hands full with my oldest brother Jerome. One day my sister went to the garden which was about 10 miles away and dug yams to sell at the market. She was in the process of taking vegetables outside. My brother passed and threw all the yams in a gutter. This brother of ours was raised with our grandfather, and was different than all of us. We had lots of problems with him as he thought he could control all the children my father left behind after his death. Even today, my sister remembers what our brother had done. Jerome collected rent from clients from rental property my sister had, but won't reimburse my sister when she visited St. Lucia. Jerome gave his girlfriend a piece of property to build a house, but he never gave my sister a penny from the rental property. He occupied younger sister's house with his girlfriend and paid nothing.

The Caribbean market sold a variety of sizes of bananas, fruits, and vegetables. My mother and other vendors sold their produce inside the market area. Fishermen went out to sea daily and caught a variety of seafood and sold in the market. Blowfish is somewhat different, as the residents roasted this fish in a charcoal pot by peeling off the skin to eat the flesh. If you like seafood, the market is where you should shop for goods when you visit the islands.

Shellfish were caught daily, but codfish was purchased in a supermarket and used in many dishes. See my recipe for fish cakes made out of codfish and spices in my cookbook Anne Marie's Family Favorite Recipes with a Caribbean Twist for more details.

Fish can be cooked in many ways such as broth, soup, fried and stewed. There are some restaurants near the market that sells Creole and French foods. The meal portions were huge, and when you order, they made sure you got enough to satisfy your appetite. They also sold callaloo soup and fried codfish.

Dasheen plant leaves could be used to make callaloo soup. This was a very popular plant which had large leaves and is grown throughout the tropics and it's an edible plant. The young leaves were cooked to make callaloo soup. Dumplings may be added to it if you want. This could be cooked as easily as potatoes. Dasheen plant had large heart-shaped leaves that grows from a short stem. The leaves were rich in vitamins and minerals.

Plantain is another popular vegetable that could be found in the market. Ripe plantains or green plantains could be cooked in different ways. There were vendors that sold various fruits such as mangoes, guavas, pineapples, plums, in different shapes and sizes, and were available in green or ripe. You could also make salads with the green mangoes. These fruits were sometimes shipped to Barbados where they make flour and shipped to London.

My family took their produce to the Farmers Market when they grew their own bananas. They also took bananas to other locations and sold in big bundles. These bananas were matured enough to get ripened and could be sold and used at your home. Today, I eat green bananas whenever it is available in the supermarket in the US.

In the United States, we do not have that luxury. Sometimes you have to go to different supermarkets in order to locate green bananas.

Every day, early in the morning, I went to the market to buy whatever I could find like fresh fish, beef liver, or flying fish, depending on what the fishermen brought back from sea. Sometimes I would fix tuna fish and pork and beans. We did not have too much electricity and used lanterns in the kitchen, living room and bedrooms. We were living close to a catholic church. I went to mass early in the morning before going to school. At my brother's house we had water flowing, but sometimes the government would turn off the water for several hours.

Later in the relationship, my boyfriend, (soon to be husband) joined the police force and went to Barbados for police training. Since my brother did not have a mailbox by his house, I went to the post office every day to send a letter to my boyfriend and then picked up a letter from him. In addition, he joined the military and the same thing happened picking up a letter every day at the post office. He was trained in the Army in Puerto Rico, then Tacoma, Washington, and then Colorado Springs, Fort Carson. He was always off base and sometimes there would be no letters. My boyfriend always falls asleep with one of my letters in his hand and the GI's were taking it from him to read.

Steps to Reverse Diabetes

Basics of Healthy Eating for Diabetes or Prediabetes

There is diabetes in our family even though we are scattered in the United States, London, England and St. Lucia, West Indies. My sister Helena and I tend to have the similar symptoms like frequent thirst and urination, always hungry, craving for sweets. When we were young and growing up, I couldn't remember anyone of us having cardiovascular disease or type 2 Diabetes. I never heard of the word Diabetes. Growing older has made a big difference. We have to watch what we eat and be careful with what we put in our mouth. As the expression goes, "you're only as old as you feel." By age 40, it was more feasible for doctors to predict whether you are a candidate for Type 2 Diabetes. I had to keep my weight down.

Type 2 Diabetes means that your body cannot use or store glucose (sugar) as it should. You may have enough insulin, but it does not work as it should to open cell walls for glucose to enter. This is called insulin resistance. It is the main problem of Type 2 Diabetes. Glucose cannot enter the cells very well and blood glucose levels rise. Your pancreas makes insulin. When blood glucose levels rise, the body responds by making extra insulin to keep blood glucose levels normal. Your pancreas works over time to make enough insulin. After years of your pancreas working extra hard, it gets tired and can no longer keep up. Insulin supply goes down and blood glucose levels goes up. This is when my Type 2 Diabetes was diagnosed.

There is no fun in injecting a person with insulin to maintain their blood sugar. For this reason, you have to control your Type 2 Diabetes the natural way by eating lots of greens, lettuce, cabbage, broccoli, and salads to control my Type 2 Diabetes and to try to reverse the condition. There are several things my doctor advised me to watch while trying to reverse your Type 2 Diabetes. This is a constant battle.

Food and Insulin

Most of the food we eat turns into sugar and enters the blood. Some foods cause your blood sugar to rise faster after you eat. Eating pizza with all the oils and fats mess up your figures quickly. Any food that has sugar in it will cause your blood sugar to rise fastest. The rise in blood sugar after a meal signals the pancreas to release the hormone, insulin. Insulin is needed to move glucose into the cells. It opens the cell walls and allows glucose to enter. Once inside the cells, glucose is burned for energy. Glucose is the fuel that your body needs to function.

Symptoms of Diabetes

I may not have any symptoms. The symptoms of Type 2 Diabetes can come on slowly, over months and even years. Symptoms could include frequent thirst for water, trips to the bathroom, urination, feeling tired, dry or itchy skin, frequent infections, slow healing, sweating while sleeping, dry mouth, numbness or tingling in toes or fingers, trouble seeing at nights.

Test Taken

My A1C test result were greater than or equal to 6.5%. Fasting blood glucose greater than equal to 126 mg/dl (fasting means nothing to eat for at least 8 hours before a blood test). Symptoms of diabetes and blood glucose of 200 mg/dL or higher.

Risk Involved

A person at the age of 40 and over, overweight, family history of Type 2 Diabetes, high blood pressure, high cholesterol, history of diabetes during pregnancy, giving birth to a 9 pounds baby, African American, Hispanic American, or Native American are good candidates to have diabetes.

Doctor Warning

In order to control your type 2 diabetes, you need to exercise in order to improve your blood sugar. If your lifestyle changes, you may need medicine to help control your blood sugar. Metformin is the first kind of medicine a doctor may offer, and treating you for prediabetes, and after that you inject insulin under your skin. Knowing about diabetes and how it's treated will help you stay healthy. I inject insulin in my stomach area where there is fat and flesh. I inject Novolog twice a day to keep my sugar down. I was prediabetic previously, but the UW Hospital decided that I should be on insulin. That decision was made between young and old doctors.

Things you have to know

How to test my blood sugar, how to eat healthy, how to eat balance meals, medicine and exercise duration, how to take medicines if needed. Learning about how to live with diabetes will help me keep my blood sugar levels controlled and stay healthy in the future. My health care team will help screen for my problems. Keep a candy bar in your purse, just in case you are too hungry to wait for real food.

I was advised to move more to stay healthy
When am I going back to the gym?

You most likely know this by now. Being active is an important part of any weight loss and weight maintenance. When you are active, your body uses more energy while burning calories. When you burn more calories than you eat, you lose weight and feel better.

Since 3,500 calories equals about one pound of fat, you need to burn 3,500 calories more than you take in to lose one pound. If you cut off 500 calories from your diet a day, you would lose one pound a week (500 x 7 = 3,500 calories). Because of changes that occur in your body all the time, calories may need to be decreased to see a better weight loss.

While some diets have more effect on weight loss than exercise, walking around has a stronger effect in preventing weight gain. For this reason, be good to yourself and follow the doctor's advice.

Aerobic activity – Get at least 150 minutes a week of moderate aerobic activity or 75 minutes a week of vigorous activity. To effectively lose and maintain weight, some people may need up to 300 minutes a week of moderate physical activity. You can also do a low impact or moderate exercise. The guidelines suggest that you spread your exercise during the week, and sessions should be at least 10 minutes in duration. At the health club, the least you work out is one hour. So, don't forget to do your workout as it is the key to maintain good health.

Strength training – do this exercise at least twice a week. Many suggest two strength training a week for 20 to 30 minutes are enough for most people, but you know your limit. The secret is to stay active.

Moderate aerobic exercise includes activities as a brisk walk, mowing the lawn, swimming, aerobic dancing. Strength training can include weight machine, gardening. The goal for these exercises is about 30 minutes every day depending on your strength. Have you taken your vitamins for today?

Care for your Diabetes

You are the most important person on the team because diabetes care and blood glucose control are really good task. My doctor, nurse educator, and dietitian will help me learn about taking care of myself. Other team members will be my dentist, eye doctor and maybe a foot doctor, as well as a counselor, and someone to help me with an exercise plan. Don't forget to include family members and friends who can support you. Follow your kids around and do whatever they do. The difference is just good and entertaining.

Are you skipping meals?

If my meals are more than 4-5 hours apart, I include a small snack. I discovered that skipping a meal makes a big difference as you eat the wrong foods. Plan your meals a day in advance or double your recipes.

Use Less Sugar and Sweets

I use water as my main drink. I can also use other sugar free drinks like crystal light with additional water. I limit fruit juices to

½ cup per day and milk to 3 cups (24 ounces) per day sometimes. The difference, when you test your blood you can tell you are doing the right thing.

Read food label ingredients. When I go to a restaurant for breakfast and ask for a small glass of juice, I also ask for an empty glass, plus a glass of water to mix and dilute the juice.

Decrease your amount of food

To create a healthy meal, we need to choose food from all food groups with less calorie intake, to get less calorie consumptions. We fill half the plate with vegetables, and limit starchy foods and grains to ¼ of the plate. This works like a charm.

Proteins

Protein foods include: Low-fat meat, chicken, fish, low-fat cheese, nuts, peanut butter, cottage cheese, and eggs. Have you tried cottage cheese with chopped apples and add a little bit of cinnamon to it? You may also add a couple walnuts. Yes, that is good stuff.

Carbohydrate foods

Carbohydrate is found in starches, fruit, milk, yogurt, and sweets. These are foods that raise blood sugar and need to be eaten in smaller portions. Tell yourself each time you are about to eat that you will not over eat.

High Fiber

I choose fresh fruits, fresh and frozen vegetables, beans, and legumes, and whole grains. "High Fiber" means a food with 3 or more grams of dietary fiber per serving.

Recommendation from primary doctor

Use less cheese, butter, margarine, oil, mayonnaise, cream, and salad dressings. Any food that is too greasy can upset your digestive system. Use salad dressings that is lower than 60 calories. Don't use much at a time.

Use non-fat or low-fat 1% milk and dairy products. Buy lean meats and remove visible fats (take skin off chicken, trim meat fat). I have been doing this for years. Limit my fatty meats to once a week or less (lunch meat, bacon, sausage, hot dogs). We bake, broil, steam, boil, or grill foods (no frying) and use nonstick cooking spray for cooking. Air Fryer is good to have in the kitchen nowadays as it eliminates calories.

- Check the blood sugar readings daily by injecting finger and my stomach
- Check your blood pressure with a cuff monitor at home, I have one
- Use **A1C** medical index for reader reference. Test to measure a person's average blood sugar level over the past two or three months. Lower blood sugar level recommended for Type 2 diabetic patients

- Lose weight if you are overweight to stay at the ideal weight
- Speak to a dietitian on simple ways to lose weight, keep watching your A1C
- Cook your meals yourself
- Diabetic medication makes you gain weight is not a myth if you don't stay active
- Doctor and nutritionist advice "stay active"
- Don't skip meals but eat three meals a day
- Don't keep junk food in your house, get enough restful sleep
- Watch what you put in your mouth
- Try Vegan and Mediterranean meals, and drink more water to quench your thirst.

Hemoglobin A1C Indication

A minor component of hemoglobin to which glucose is found. Abbreviated HbA1c. HbA1c levels depend on the blood glucose: The higher the glucose in blood, the higher the level of HbA1c. Levels of HbA1c are not influenced by daily fluctuations in the blood glucose, but reflect the average glucose levels over the prior 6 to 8 weeks. Measurement of HbA1c is an indication because it informs how well the blood level has been in the past, and may be used to monitor the effects of diet, exercise, and therapy on patients with diabetes. The A1C needs to stay down, otherwise your doctor will talk to you about it. This is the time you really watch your eating habits if you know you will be tested.

In healthy people without diabetes, sometimes the HbA1c level is less than 7% of total hemoglobin. This author's AbA1c level is 6.4%. This author has achieved this AbA1c level by going to the health club to do exercise activities, etc. anything that elevates your blood pressure, working on health rider bikes. The author has several exercise videos on belly dancing, walking outside or on the park playground, dancing with Caribbean groups, walk in the neighborhood, sidewalks, dancing on Magic 98 Radio Station music.

Cardiovascular disease, also known as heart disease, affects the family. In recent years doctors have gained significant insight into what causes heart diseases, and what medicine to prescribe for the condition. You may not be aware of what it means to live with diabetes and heart disease. Eating healthy is the key for reducing Type 2 Diabetes and health complications. Unfortunately, there are no miracle foods that can lower blood sugar. We need a moderate amount of sugar in our system, but we have to be careful with the amount of sugar we use today.

A person with heart disease must stay active unless a doctor advises you otherwise. Those who live with diabetes and heart disease, operate on a different lifestyle. This can lead to complications such as blood pressure, blood clots, stroke, heart attack and seizures. This is true as this author lost two brothers from heart attacks.

You need to participate in physical activities like walking, dancing, playing ball games. Stay active to improve your blood circulation and strengthen the muscles in your body. This will encourage a sense of wellness and healthiness. If you are living with diabetes and heart disease, go out and walk around the park at least 30 minutes a day like my brother Denis does every day. At the park some places have several pieces of exercise equipment that you can work on. My brother may have the symptoms of diabetes, but his doctor assured him that he does not have the condition. Don't just sit in the house. You can also play with your children. Give it a try and ride your bike to work.

Low Blood Sugar Reading: Less than 70

You are at an increased risk of having low blood sugar if you take certain diabetes medications? Some people wear a medical jewelry indicating that they have diabetes. Use bracelets with insignia indicating your disease. There are things you and your family and friends need to know. Do not stay hungry, eat when you can, but do not over indulge before going to bed. Eat your heavy meals earlier in the day and eat less in the evening so you can sleep better, then watch what happen.

Causes: Not eating enough carbohydrates, delaying or skipping meals, too much diabetes medication, extra activity, (especially without food) Onset: Sudden, may progress quickly. Symptoms include:

Anxiety	• Stress that can result from work, school, personal relationship emotional trauma.

Impaired Vision	Visual impairment, also known as vision impairment or vision loss, **is a** decreased ability to see to a degree that causes problems not fixable by usual means, such as glasses. Visual impairment is often defined as a best corrected visual acuity of worse than either 20/40 or 20/60.
Shaking	Move (an object) up and down or from side to side with rapid, forceful, jerky movements. **"she stood in the hall and shook her umbrella"**
Sweating	Sweating is a bodily function that helps regulate your body's temperature. Also called perspiration, sweating is the release of a salt-based fluid from your sweat glands. Changes in your body.
Weakness/ Fatigue	Weakness is a lack of physical or muscle strength and the feeling that extra effort is required to move your arms, legs, or other muscles. Fatigue is a feeling of tiredness or exhaustion or a need to rest because of lack of energy or you are tired.
Irritability	A tendency to get excited, angry or upset easily. No patience.
Dizziness	Central dizziness is caused by problems in the balance portion of the brain. Anytime this portion of the brain is not working properly, dizziness can occur. Symptoms usually include lightheadedness, disorientation, imbalance, and sometimes even blacking out.

Hunger	Hunger is a condition in which a person, for a sustained period, is unable to eat sufficient food to meet basic nutritional needs. So, in the field of hunger relief, the term hunger is used in a sense that goes beyond the common desire for food.

What to do:

1. Check your blood sugar. If you are 70 or below, that is too low.
2. When treating low blood sugar, avoid chocolate, ice cream, candy bars or sweets, these take too long to act. Do treat with a quick acting sugar equaling about 15 grams of carbohydrate:
   - 4 glucose tablets
   - ½ cup orange juice
   - 5 life savers or candies
   - 1 cup milk
   - 1 tablespoon honey, regular syrup, regular sugar
   - 2 tablespoons raisins
3. If you do not feel back to normal, always test after 15 minutes. If less than 70, repeat step 2
4. When your blood sugar is greater than 70, if possible, get your next meal within an hour. If that is not possible, eat a light snack such as 1/2 a sandwich with 4 oz. milk.

Safety Reminders

- Never drive or go back to sleep without retesting
- Low blood sugar can lead to a medical emergency if not treated
- If you are unconscious, unable to swallow or having seizures, a family member or friend should call 911.

The story is a myth: Overweight people get diabetes

When you are overweight or obese, this increases the chances of getting diabetes, and that is a risk factor. Genetics, age, and family history can play a vital role in your condition.

The majority of overweight people won't develop diabetes, and many people with Type 2 Diabetes are not overweight. It does not matter how much you weigh. Keep track of your readings and numbers like this author does. My nutritionist calls frequently to find out my numbers to evaluate me.

Eating Protein

Everyone has heard about high protein diets. This provides greater feeling of fullness than the other nutrients. In fact, eating breakfast makes you less hungry during the day. Choose protein rich food sources that will help you feel full, but will also be healthy for your body.

Health officials agree that people who eat protein throughout the day don't eat as much. Doctors want you to choose protein sources that will help you feel full, but will be healthy for your body.

We need to select lean protein and healthy portions of these foods in your snacks and meals. For example, a terrific snack would be an apple with 1 tablespoon peanut butter, or a slice of whole wheat bread with a slice of low-fat cheese or ½ cup of plain yogurt.

Healthy Snack Try one of these Proteins

1 oz. low-fat cheese

3 hard-boiled egg whites (or 1 hard-boiled egg)

10 almonds

1 tablespoon peanut butter

1 slice turkey

1 small veggie burger (12-oz patty)

½ regular size can of tuna in water

½ cup cottage cheese

3 scrambled egg whites

20 soy nuts

1/3 of a protein bar (these are high in calories so you don't need the whole bar!)

Example of Healthy Meal Proteins

3-oz grilled chicken

4-oz grilled fish (no breading/crust)

4-oz tofu

1 larger veggie burger (4-5 oz patty)

3-oz lean steak or pork (no ribs)

3-oz ground turkey burger, 1 can tuna fish or salmon

Food	Serving	Fiber Grams
Fresh and Dried Fruit		
Pear	1 medium	5.1
Dry Figs	2 media	3.7
Fresh blueberries	1 cup	3.5
Apple with peel	1 medium	3.3
Dried peaches	3 halves	3.3
Dried apricots	10 halves	2.6
Orange	1 medium	3.1
Raisins	1.5 oz box	1.6
Fresh Strawberries	1 cup	3.0

Example of Healthy Complex Carbs		
Whole wheat pasta	1 cup cooked	6.3
Unsweetened bran cereal	¾ cup	5.3
Oatmeal	1 cup cooked	4.1

Food	Serving	Fiber Grams
Whole wheat bread	1 slice	1.5 – 3.0
Lentils	1 cup cooked	15.6
Black beans	1 cup cooked	15.0
Lima beans	1 cup cooked	13.0
Chick peas	½ cup	6.2
Peas	1 cup cooked	8.8
Brussels sprouts	1 cup cooked	6.4
Baked potato with skin	1 medium	4.4
Turnip greens	1 cup boiled	5.0
Spinach	1 cup boiled/ steamed	4.3
Broccoli	1 cup boiled/ steamed	4.7
String beans	1 cup boiled/ steamed	4.0

The rule of thumb is that the less refined or processed a food is, and the more fiber it contains, the more it will help you with hunger control and weight loss in moderate portions.

Protein Eating Tips:

You can incorporate protein into your goals by committing to having at least one protein at all snacks and meals for one week.

Select from the snack protein and meal protein list and make sure you have these foods on hand.

- **Vegetables:** They are a source of fiber and many different vitamins and minerals. Eating more than five fruits and vegetables a day can significantly reduce the risk of heart disease.

- **Carrots:** What makes them so good and special? Eating raw vegetables, such as carrots and broccoli, helps make for comfortable bowel movements. However, eating cooked carrots may be better for absorption of carotenoids which become more bioavailable once vegetables have been heated. A study found that cooked, pureed carrots, had higher antioxidant capacity than their raw counterparts. So, eat them both raw and cooked.

- **Cashews:** Cashew shells grows at the end of the sweet-flavored cashew apple which is often used in the Caribbean islands and to make jams and chutneys. The apple that bears the cashew is really called "pome" and comes in a yellow color. When it is ripe, it is sweet like a pear. In order to cook the cashew, you roast it, at that time it has no salt added to its flavor. Cashew nut processing prepares the cashew nut for consumption. In most basic form, cashew nut processing involves the removal of the cashew shell from the meaty nut, washing the nut to rid it of any foreign matter, then soaking and roasting it. Once this process is completed, the cashew nuts are ready to be eaten.

- **Legumes:** Legumes include beans, peas, lentils and chickpeas, and they are all rich in fiber and protein. A number of studies have shown that eating legumes is associated with lower mortality.

- **Whole grains:** Whole grains are also rich in fiber. A high intake of whole grains can reduce blood pressure and death from heart disease.

- **Nuts:** Nuts are great sources of fiber, protein, and polyunsaturated and monounsaturated fats. Combined with healthy diet, they are associated with reduced mortality.

- **For example**, fish is often eaten all over the world. It is a good source of omega-3 which is important for the heart and brain.

- **Eating fish** is associated with slower brain decline in old age and reduced heart disease.

- **Potassium** is an essential nutrient. Potassium is important for blood pressure control and may improve heart health.

- Eat a 95% plant-base diet that's rich in legumes, whole grains, vegetables and nuts, all of which can help reduce the risk of death.

- Chronic diseases are becoming more and more common in old age. Everything starts to happen. Swelling of the face, feet, knees, stomach.

- **Watermelon:** Slices of watermelon fills you up and can help you lose weight. You don't get hungry as fast, but it makes you go to the bathroom. It also helps keep your blood pressure down.

- Look for a melon that is dark green, heavy for its size and uniform shape.
- When this author visited her doctor's office on June 4, 2019, her blood pressure was perfect 121/78 because she had been eating watermelon. Prior to that, her blood pressure had been higher with 145/82.
- **Zucchini:** A perfect weight loss food, low in calories, and high in fiber and vitamin C. A diet high in potassium and low in sodium can help keep blood pressure down. When buying zucchini, look for the very small ones. Large ones can be tough and seedy. The small and medium have better flavor. Did you know that one cup of cooked zucchini has potassium as much as a ripe banana?

While genetics somewhat determine your lifespan and susceptibility to these diseases, your lifestyle probably has a greater impact. Once you set your goal, write it down and carve to work on it. Committing to spending time on your goal to achieve it.

The Best Diet for Type 2 Diabetes – Overview

If you live with Type 2 Diabetes, eating a well-balanced diet can help manage your blood sugar levels and weight. If your meal plan helps you to achieve a healthier weight and keep your blood sugar levels in a normal range, it may reduce your risk for complications.

Foods needed to maintain a proper and healthy diet

Foods with less calories

5 cups chopped lettuce	Cooked Portion
1 cup shredded cabbage	1 ½ cup broccoli 8 oz.
1 medium tomato	1 ½ kale 7 oz.
1 small carrot	
¼ cup raw onion	

Lunch and dinner recipes can be used at one. When you have leftovers, they can be substituted for other meals. If you like a recipe, double or triple it and freeze individual portions. You don't have to cook every day. Eat less bread. Don't have a breakfast meal more than once a day it depends on the individual.

Frozen vegetables or fruits can be substituted for fresh. Don't use canned vegetables or fruit. Canned products lose its nutrients during processing and often contain added sugar or salt. Rinse your canned vegetables and fruits to remove sugar and sodium.

There are many different eating patterns and diets that you can follow to meet your health needs. When you are deciding which one is right for you, consider going through this checklist of questions below:

Does this eating plan include a wide variety of nutrient-rich foods?

To meet your body's needs, it's important to eat a colorful array of nutrient-dense foods. For example, fruits, vegetables, beans and other legumes, nuts and seeds, whole grains, and fish are good sources of vitamins and minerals, as well as fiber.

How to Read Food Labels

When you go grocery shopping, take time to read the nutrition labels on your purchases. Compare nutrients and calories in one food to those in another. The information may surprise you. Select what suits you for your diet.

One easy way to do "healthier" grocery shopping is to make a list at home before going to the supermarket and stick to it.

Most foods in the grocery store must now have a nutrition label and list of ingredients. Claims like "low cholesterol" and "fat free" can be used only if a food meets legality set by the government. The nutritional fats label includes the following types of information:

Serving

If you eat double the serving size listed, you need to double the calories, fat and nutrients. If you eat half the size shown, cut the calories down and nutrients in half.

Type of Fat

Most people need to cut back on calories and fat. Too much fat may contribute to heart disease. The label gives you the number of grams of fat per serving (so you can track your daily intake) and the number of calories from fat. The label can be misleading or incomprehensible. If you are overweight or trying to lose weight, your goal is an overall intake of no more than 25 to 35 percent of your total calories from fat. You should keep track of the number of calories you consume and the amounts of calories you burn.

Saturated Fat

Saturated fat has fatty acid. This is one part of the total fat in food. It is the key nutrient for raising your blood cholesterol and your risk of heart disease and stroke. Consume less saturated fats.

Cholesterol Level

Too much of it in your diet is not good. Too much cholesterol in your blood can lead to heart disease and stroke. Does your doctor send you a letter after testing your blood levels? This is another way to watch your cholesterol and medication. Have you heard of anyone with heart blockage? Watch your fat intake.

Sodium

Watch for both natural and added sodium. Ordinary table salt is sodium chloride – 40 percent sodium by weight. Healthy adults should take in less sodium each day. That's equal to about 1 teaspoon of salt. Some people – African Americans, middle-aged and older adults, and people with high blood pressure – need less sodium per day. The salt prolongs the water in your system.

Fiber is an important part of your diet. This will show what fiber is, where it's found, and how to increase the amount of fiber in your diet.

Compare these two meal plans. Which one is most like your diet?

Menu low in Fiber Breakfast	Menu high in fiber Breakfast
Orange Juice	Fresh whole orange
Scrambled Eggs	Scrambled eggs
White toast	Oat Bran Muffin
Margarine	Margarine
Milk	Milk
Lunch	**Lunch**
Tomato Soup	Minestrone Soup

½ tuna salad sandwich on white bread	½ tuna salad sandwich on wheat bread
Fudge brownie	Fresh Strawberries
Milk	Milk
Dinner	**Dinner**
Baked Chicken	Chicken/Broccoli stir-fry
Buttered Noodles	Brown Rice
Green Beans	Fresh Fruit Salad
Butterscotch Pudding	Apple Crisp
Milk	Milk

Fruits are grouped by the average amount of fiber in a serving. The fruits are fresh unless otherwise indicated. The serving size is ½ cup.

High Fiber Fruits

Over 3 grams fiber per serving		2.1-3.0 grams fiber per serving	
Prunes, 5 dried	3.1	Blueberries	2.1
Raisins	3.2	Orange, 1 medium	2.2
Apple, 1 lg, unpeeled	3.6	Apple, 1 lg, peeled	2.6
Avocado, ½	3.8	Raspberries	2.6
Dates, 3 dried	4.3		
Pear, 1 unpeeled	4.7		
Blackberries	4.9		

Low Fiber Fruits			
1.1-2.0 grams fiber per serving		**Under 1-gram fiber per serving**	
Apricots, 4 halves fresh, canned or dried	1.3	Fruit juices	.2
Strawberries	1.4	Mandarin oranges	.3
Peach, peeled	1.4	Watermelon	.3
Cherries, sweet	1.5	Grapefruit sections	.4
Mango	1.5	Olives, 5 green or black	.4
Applesauce, cooked	1.5	Friar & prune plum, 1	.5
Tangerine,1 medium	1.5	Honeydew melon	.5
Nectarine, 2-1/2"	1.6	Grapes, green or red	.5
Pears, 2 peeled halves	1.7	Cantaloupe	.6
Banana, (8-3/4" long)	1.9	Pineapple	.7
		Cherries, sour canned	.8
		Fruit cocktail, canned	.9

Vegetables

Vegetables are grouped by the average amount of fiber in a serving. The serving size is ½ c. fresh vegetable unless otherwise noted. My sister Helena got very small by cutting down on meat and fat. She would not eat meat, fish, or chicken for a long time, until her doctor asked her to stop for a while. My sister ate bread and lettuce as her meal, and now she is smaller than myself. My husband saw my sister on my cell and asked who is that. This makes a big difference as my sister drank lots of water and watched what she ate while taking care of her diabetes 2.

Note: Sometimes there appears to be a discrepancy between the amount of fiber in a cooked verses fresh vegetable (e.g. mushrooms). There is often a greater volume of vegetable in a ½ c. cooked portion compared to a ½ c. raw portion, therefore, there is more fiber in ½ c. cooked mushrooms or spinach compared to ½ c. raw.

High Fiber Vegetables

Over 3 grams fiber per serving		2.1-3.0 grams fiber per serving	
Brussels sprouts	3.1	Mushrooms, canned	2.0
Pumpkin, canned	3.5	Carrot, 1 lg	2.1
Potato with skin, 1 lg	4.7	Turnip greens, cooked	2.1
Lima beans, cooked	5.1	Rhubarb, cooked	2.2
Pork & beans, cooked	5.6	Spinach, cooked	2.3
Kidney beans, cooked	6.6	Spinach, raw, 2 c.	2.3
		Broccoli	2.7
		Green beans	2.8

Low Fiber Vegetables

1.1-2.0 grams fiber per serving		Under 1-gram fiber per serving	
Peppers	1.1	Mushrooms, fresh	.3
Celery	1.4	Lettuce, iceberg/leaf	.4

Onions	1.5	Chinese cabbage	.4
Green beans	1.5	Cucumber, peeled	.5
Cauliflower	1.5	Radish	.6
Asparagus	1.5	Zucchini	.7
Sweet potatoes, peeled	1.6	Cabbage, raw	.7
		Bean sprouts	.8
		Tomato, ½ c. canned 2-1/2" fresh	.8
		Potatoes, peeled	.9

Bread, Cereal, Rice and Pasta

The Nutrition Facts information on food labels will list fiber content.

High Fiber Foods	
Bran, including oat and wheat bran	Rye flour
Brown rice	Soybean flour
Buckwheat	Wild rice
Oatmeal	Whole wheat flour
Foods made with whole oats	Breads labeled "healthy" or
Peanut flour	mixed grain breads

Cereals

Read food labels and choose high fiber cereals. Cereals that contain 5 grams of fiber or more are considered high fiber.

What is Fiber?

Fiber is a component of plant foods that is indigestible. There are two types.

- Insoluble fibers or "roughage", are found in fruit and vegetable skins and in the bran layer of whole wheat.
- Soluble fibers form a gel in water. Good sources include citrus fruit, barley, oatmeal, oat bran and dried peas and beans.

Dietary Fiber

Fruits, vegetables, whole grains, peas and beans are good sources and can help reduce the risk of heart disease.

Protein

Where there is animal protein, there is also fat and cholesterol. Eat small portions.

Vitamins and Multivitamins

Eating a variety of foods will help you reach your daily goal of 100 percent of vitamin A, vitamin C, calcium and iron.

Daily Value

The daily values are guides for people who eat 2,000 calories each day. If you eat more or less than that, your daily value may be higher or lower. Choose foods with a low percentage daily value of fat, saturated fat, cholesterol and sodium. Try to reach 100 percent of the daily value of total carbohydrates, dietary fiber, vitamins and minerals.

Do you Have Any Shopping Ideas?

Cutting back on sodium or eating more fruits and vegetables, do you have grocery shopping tips or recipes you use to help you eat healthfully? Drink more water to curb hunger. Make a list of your grocery in advance before you go to the supermarket. Each time you ran out of a product at home, write it down on the list so you do not purchase what you really don't need in the supermarket.

Overeating Difficulties

Overeating can spoil your thought on how to maintain a normal blood sugar level. It would also increase your weight. Taking foods with high-fiber can leave you full for a longer period. You may choose most fruits and vegetables, and whole grains.

Duration of eating plans

Healthy eating plans only work if you follow them. If your plan is too restrictive or does not fit your lifestyle, it can be hard to stick with. If you love a certain food and can't imagine life without it, make sure you select a meal plan that allows you to have it at least occasionally or once a week.

What foods a person with diabetes can't have

There are only few foods that you need to avoid when you have a Type 2 Diabetes. But some foods are a healthier choice – they are a rich source of minerals and vitamins, less sugar, fat, salt and cholesterol. When baking cookies, use only half of what is required on the recipe and reduce the fat content. Just remember that sugar is sweet, so try to control the amount used.

- **Foods low in cholesterol**. That means avoiding foods that are high in cholesterol, such as red meat, egg yolks, high-fat dairy products, and other animal products.
- **Foods low in added sugars.** That means limiting sweetened drinks, candy, desserts, and being cautious about processed foods.

Foods that contain carbohydrates

- Wheat, and other grains and grain-based foods
- Dried beans, lentils, and other legumes

- Potatoes and other starchy vegetables
- Fruit and fruit juices
- Milk and yogurt
- Processed snack foods, desserts, and sweetened beverages

So, What Happens if you Have Type 2 Diabetes?

Your body can't keep your blood sugar levels within normal limits. This happens because the cells are not able to use insulin. The pancreas is not able to produce enough insulin. You need external sources of insulin to keep your levels stable. Each time your A1C has to be tested, blood has to be drawn by a lab to perform that test.

If you have Type 2 Diabetes, you may already be on insulin. Insulin helps you maintain your target blood sugar levels. If you are new to insulin therapy, you might find the treatment challenging.

Who Should Take Insulin?

Insulin is not prescribed to all people with Type 2 Diabetes. Most doctors prescribe metformin as the first-line drug in managing Type 2 Diabetes. Your doctor may prescribe oral medications if metformin isn't helping you maintain your target blood sugar levels. Doctors don't change your medication easily.

Long lasting insulin mimics the action of basal insulin in the body. This type of insulin is often the first type used. It is consistent in maintaining the blood sugar levels during extended periods and fasting. Basal insulin works with other types of diabetes medication. Basal insulin is also called Lantus (Glargine).

According to the doctors and nutritionists who watch a patient dealing with Type 2 Diabetes, they advised not sharing your Lantus pen with other people, even if the needle has been changed. You may give another person a serious infection, or get a serious infection from them.

- Severe allergic reaction (whole body reaction). Get medical help right away if you have any of these signs or symptoms of severe allergic reaction:
- A rash over your whole body, trouble breathing, a fast heartbeat, or sweating.
- Get emergency medical help if you have:
- Trouble breathing, shortness of breath, fast heartbeat, swelling of your face, tongue, or throat, sweating, extreme drowsiness, dizziness, confusion.

Where should I inject the insulin?

You can inject insulin anywhere in your body as long as there is a fat layer under the skin to inject into. The best sites for injection include the abdomen, back of your arms, and outer thighs.

It is important to rotate your injection sites.

Otherwise, scar tissues may develop if you inject in the same spot all the time. Also, do not inject too close to the belly button.

Should I work with a diabetes educator?

Some people can get away without the help of a diabetes educator, so should you get one? This is a personal question, and one you should discuss with your family, friends, and doctor. A diabetes educator can help you with your management plan and can help you develop one you can stick to.

Your doctor can refer you to a diabetes educator or you can look for one at the nearest health center. You don't have to work with a diabetes educator daily but at least every three to six months per year.

But until you feel comfortable with your treatment plan, you will need to see them as a resource for when you have high readings, they are good help and they may have a doctor available to ask questions. You will need to see your diabetes educator at least twice a year. This way, they can check your progress and if you are doing very well, they can change your medication.

Should I change my lifestyle following my treatment?

You will need to decide on how to change your lifestyle once you begin your insulin treatment. It is important to manage your blood sugar level with diet, even if you take medication. When you are on insulin, you need to be sure to manage when and how much carbohydrate you take in. This will help you avoid blood sugar levels becoming too low or too high. This is something your diabetes educator or dietitian or doctor can help you with.

Exercise is very important. It lowers blood sugar levels and reduces your risk for heart disease. But if you are taking insulin, make sure to time your exercise, and manage the intensity. Make sure you check with your doctor for information on when to exercise. Also, find out what form of exercise is best for you.

Ways that sugary soda is bad for your health

Here are the reasons why sugary soda is bad for your health. Sugar-sweetened beverages are the most fattening and most harmful aspect of the diet.

Humalog vs. Novolog

Humalog and Novolog are rapid acting types of insulin. Learn their similarities and differences.

What Can I Drink If I have Diabetes?

If you have diabetes, grabbing something to drink may not be as simple as reaching into the fridge. Ditch the guessing game and reach for a glass of water, or decaffeinated tea.

All About the Hemoglobin A1C Test

The A1C test for diabetes allows doctors to see glucose levels over a two to three-month period. It is used to monitor blood sugar level. You have to fast before testing your blood for A1C test.

Low Blood Sugar (Hypoglycemia)

Hypoglycemia, or low blood sugar, is a potentially dangerous condition that is most common in people with diabetes: Symptoms are sudden and range from mild to severe. Excessive sweating, tiredness, lightheadedness, feeling dizzy and weak, a sudden feeling of excess hunger, increased heart rate, blurred vision, confusion, irritable or nervous.

Symptoms of hypoglycemia during sleep include: Having nightmares, crying in sleep, excessive sweating so as to dampen your clothes, feeling tired, irritated or confused after waking up.

Ripe vs. Unripe Bananas: Which are better for you

Surprising Green Banana benefits you probably didn't know. My sister buys green bananas, cook, and freeze it and use at a later time. Would you like to try? This author eats plenty green bananas at home.

✓ Most people tend to skip over the unripen or green bananas, but did you know that there are actually a ton of benefits with consuming green bananas?

✓ Keep watching to find out how you could benefit from eating these unripen and delicious fruits.

✓ Unripen bananas have a high amount of starch and fiber, which can help prevent any type of bloating and constipation during digestion.

✓ They will regulate blood pressure.

- ✓ Bananas are high in potassium which is extremely important for lowering the stress levels of your arteries and blood vessels.
- ✓ Eating green bananas can lower the tension caused by higher blood pressure levels.
- ✓ If you are able to eat bananas, it's important to be mindful of the ripeness and size of the banana to reduce its effect on your blood sugar level. Buy small ones.
- ✓ Eating green bananas have short-chain fatty acids which help improve how well your body absorb nutrients.
- ✓ This in turn, will help improve the overall health of your colon.
- ✓ Unripen bananas contain a large number of essential vitamins and minerals that your body needs to operate efficiently.
- ✓ They boost your metabolism.
- ✓ This includes complex carbohydrates which your body needs for energy.
- ✓ They can also help speed up how quickly your body burns calories.
- ✓ Green bananas contain almost forty percent of the recommended daily value of vitamin B6.
- ✓ This critical vitamin helps form hemoglobin, aids in blood sugar control, and plays a major role in hundreds of reactions in your body.
- ✓ A raw banana can help maintain the balance of electrolytes within your body. This will help keep your kidney functioning properly and kidney issues.

- ✓ Green bananas are a great option for diabetics who still want to consume bananas without their sugar content.
- ✓ They are great for diabetics.
- ✓ Fully yellow bananas and ones with brown spots have a higher sugar content, so these should be avoided.
- ✓ Although eating unripen bananas does seem unappealing, you can always boil them, fry them, or put them into shakes to make them easier to consume.
- ✓ They are really no difference unripe when they are ripe, just that they may be a bit more bitter and definitely a lot less sweet.
- ✓ When it comes to bananas, many of us think only a monkey likes bananas. Eating two green bananas every day for a week and this will happen.
- ✓ They have a ton of important vitamins and minerals and offer different health benefits for our bodies.
- ✓ If we are going to eat green bananas, they will need to be boiled or fried first, with boiled generally being a healthier choice.
- ✓ Let's discuss the health benefits of green bananas and how they can be important health benefits to your diet.
- ✓ Rather than being broken down by our bodies, it will pass through the intestines unchanged, similar to the characteristics of insoluble fiber.
- ✓ By consuming this resistant starch regularly, this can offer a number of important health benefits.
- ✓ It can provide several changes to our metabolism and reduce fat storage while also increasing the rate of fat

burning since it may block the ability of the body to use carbohydrates as fuel.

✓ It can also improve insulin sensitivity while decreasing glycemic and insulin responses.

✓ This can be beneficial for those individuals with Type 2 Diabetes.

✓ Also, it can lower plasma cholesterol and triglyceride concentrations in the body which can promote our overall health.

✓ Another reason to enjoy green bananas is that they are full of healthy fiber. One cup of boiled green bananas contains about 3.6 grams of fiber.

✓ They have a ton of important vitamins and minerals and offer different health benefits for our bodies.

✓ We commonly choose to eat ripe bananas because of this and because of their taste, but did not know that eating unripe bananas also has many health benefits?

✓ Importantly, if we are going to eat green bananas, they will need to be boiled or fried first, with boiled generally being the healthier choice.

✓ One benefit that green bananas have over yellow bananas is that they are "starchier". More specifically, they contain resistant starch.

✓ This is a type of starch that is not digested the same way as other starches are.

✓ This will help with the proper functioning of the digestive tract and overall digestion.

- ✓ It can also make you feel full, which is important for those individuals who are trying to lose weight.
- ✓ It can also promote healthy bowel movement and again be beneficial for those individuals with diabetes.
- ✓ By consuming this resistant starch regularly, this can offer a number of important health benefits.
- ✓ Green bananas are a great food choice for the "good" bacteria that is in our bodies.
- ✓ These bacteria that are found in our intestines will be able to benefit from the resistant starch that is found in green bananas, helping to keep the digestive tract and stomach healthy.
- ✓ The good intestinal bacteria will ferment the resistant starch and then use it to make energy, helping to get rid of unwanted bad bacteria.
- ✓ It also will produce short-chain fatty acids that help to keep the colon healthy and allows us to absorb nutrients from the healthy foods we eat better.
- ✓ Green bananas, just like yellow bananas are high in a number of vitamins and minerals. They are a great source of potassium.
- ✓ One cup of boiled green bananas contains about 531 mgs of potassium. They also contain good amounts of vitamin C and B vitamins.
- ✓ To prepare green bananas, place the whole, unpeeled banana into a pot of boiling water.

- ✓ It is often recommended that you let them boil for about 20 minutes or until they are soft enough to be pierced with a fork easily.
- ✓ Now remove it from the boiling water. You will be able to easily remove the peel since it will be soft.
- ✓ Another way to peel a banana is to use a knife and remove the skin and boil in a pan of water for 20 minutes with no sweat. This works better too.
- ✓ When it comes to bananas, many of us go well … literally "bananas" for them; after all they are the nation's favorite fruit, and the original 100 calorie snack! Sometimes we often look at a fruit and think "oh, it's far too ripe" or "oh shucks, that fruit is too green!" which is a shame because quite often, different stages of a fruit's maturity have different benefits.

The other popular vegetable in the Caribbean is yam. They grow white and yellow yams. The yellow yam is somewhat bitter, but also starchy. When you eat these yams in the evening, you won't get hungry in a hurry. Another favorite vegetable in the Caribbean is called cush-cush. It is very soft when cooked and can be eaten with fish, meat, or chicken and gravy. Actually, the cush-cush melts in your mouth.

SLEEP APNEA

This Author had a habit of watching TV late and could not sleep at nights. Doctors suggested CPAP to correct the problem. Usually she would sleep two hours a night with CPAP machine, but now machine gives a better report of 8:45 sometimes and that eliminated sleep problem. Normally, a medical doctor recommends that procedure for its patient to receive the treatment for sleep apnea after it is diagnosed. First, the author slept at a Sleep Clinic, while a nurse monitors her sleep pattern. If the sleep was not sufficient the first time, another test is done. If that second sleep test was not good enough, treatment is prescribed by a respiratory therapist. Then CPAP equipment is used and monitored on a humidifier machine. Both Unity Point at Home and the Sleep Clinic administers this procedure, while the patient sleeps to maintain a reasonable record. In other words, this requires patient to have health insurance to cover the expenses. Unity selects a face mask to be used by the patient. The patient needs to sleep at least four hours at nights in order to keep the humidifier after the end of six months.

Your mind also processes and responds to important emotion and experiences from the day and commits them to memory. Sleep is also essential to regulating your emotions and blood pressure. In fact, being sleep deprived for just one night can increase your emotional response to negative feelings by 60%. Unity selects a face mask for you to sleep with to get better health.

A lack of sleep makes it difficult for your body to regulate essential things like appetite control, your immune system, good metabolic function and your ability to maintain a normal body weight, and even your blood pressure.

Lastly, sleep plays an important role in regulating your internal clock. This inner clock runs on an approximately 24-hour schedule and regulates when you feel awake and sleepy. It may also help regulate things like metabolism, immune function and inflammation. Not sleeping long enough, sleeping at odd times of the day and exposure to bright light at night may throw off this inner clock and the many processes it regulates. While you may think you are getting ample rest, not all sleep is created equal. Not only is it important to get enough sleep each night, but it is also important to get good quality sleep. Nevertheless, there is no universal definition for sleep quality.

However, it may be defined as how long it takes you to fall asleep, how often you wake up during the night, how rested you feel the next day or how much time you spend in different stages of sleep.

Because good sleep is necessary to so many aspects of good health, you should make getting enough sleep each night a high priority. Getting enough quality sleep is necessary for various reasons, including maintaining your immune system and metabolic function, processing the day's memories and maintaining a normal body weight.

How much Sleep you need depends on Several Things?

Every individual has unique needs and preferences, and the answer to how much sleep you need is no different. Nevertheless, the amount of sleep you need per night is largely determined by your age. Official recommendations for sleep duration are broken down by age group:

- Older adults (65+):7-8 hours
- Adults (18-64 years): 7-9 hours
- Teenagers (14-17 years): 8-10 hours
- School children (6-13 years): 9-11 hours
- Preschoolers (3-5 years): 10-13 hours
- Toddlers (1-2 years): 11-14 hours
- Infants (4-11 months): 12-15 hours
- Newborns (0-3 months): 14-17 hours

However, some people might need more or less sleep than is generally recommended, depending on their genetic factors.

Certain genetic mutations can affect how long you need to sleep, at what time of day you prefer to sleep and how you respond to sleep deprivation. Unfortunately, your genetic makeup is not something you can change, and there is no practical way to know if you carry one of these mutations.

The new guidelines stress the importance of using proper technique to measure blood pressure. Blood pressure levels should be based on an average of two to three readings on at least two different occasions the authors said.

Healthy Meals – Try These Easy Meal Ideas You Can Make in Just Minutes

If you're like most people, convenience is a factor when choosing what to eat — but grab-and-go foods aren't always the best choices. The next time you need a quick and easy meal idea, try one of these healthy meals that you can whip up in minutes:

Begin with	Add	For
Prewashed salad greens	Shredded rotisserie chicken, sliced tomatoes, and a splash of your favorite reduced-fat dressing or a little olive oil and balsamic vinegar	Chicken salad

Whole-wheat pasta, cooked according to the manufacturer's directions	Microwaved in-the-bag mixed vegetables, topped with prepared marinara sauce and sprinkled with shredded Parmesan cheese	Quick pasta primavera

Whole-grain tortillas	Fat-free refried beans and reduced-fat shredded cheddar cheese, microwaved to melt the cheese, topped with salsa and folded	Bean burritos
Baked large baking potatoes	Heated canned vegetarian chili and a sprinkle of reduced-fat cheese	Baked chili potatoes
Microwaved prepackaged brown rice	Frozen stir-fry vegetables and strips of chicken, stir-fried in a small amount of oil	Stir-fried chicken and vegetables over rice
Toasted whole-wheat buns	Heated lean roast-beef slices from the deli, reduced-fat cheese and veggies	Roast beef sandwich
Toasted whole-wheat hoagie buns	Lettuce leaves, tuna salad made with a small amount of mayonnaise and your favorite veggie toppings	Tuna sub sandwich

EXERCISE PLAN
AND SCHEDULE

Whether you're just starting an exercise program or have been exercising for years, the most important points to know about exercise are:

1) All exercise adds up.
2) Pick exercise that you enjoy and will stick with.
3) The time of day you exercise is not important, but fitting it into your schedule is.
4) Exercise at a challenging yet comfortable level that's right for you.

Pick Exercise You Enjoy

There are so many exercise choices, but it is important picking something you'll stick with, which means picking something you enjoy. Whether you enjoy treadmill, jogging, bicycling, aerobic dance, strength training, interval training or enjoying the outdoors, pick activities that match your likes and lifestyle.

Six 30-minute workouts = 180 minutes

Three 60-minute workouts = 180 minutes

Three 30-minute workouts + one 40-minute workout + one-50-minute workout = 180 minutes.

Exercise at a Challenging yet Comfortable Level

Everyone's fitness level is different, and therefore exercise at a level that is right for you. When you exercise, you should be working out at an intensity level that is challenging, yet comfortable. This means that you should push yourself, challenge yourself, but not to the point of pain. If you experience pain or discomfort, then stop or modify your exercise to a level that is challenging yet comfortable.

Determining Your Target Heart Rate

To determine your heart rate during exercise, take your pulse by placing 2 fingers (pointer and index) on either of your wrists or the side of your neck. Count the number of beats for 10 seconds using the seconds on the clock or watch to keep time. Multiply that number by 6 to get your beats per minute.

Use the table below to find your age and determine whether you are exercising in your Target Heart Rate Zone.

Age	Target HR Zone for Moderate Intensity
20 years	100-170 beats per minute
25 years	98-166 beats per minute
30 years	95-162 beats per minute
35 years	93-157 beats per minute
40 years	90-153 beats per minute
45 years	88-149 beats per minute
50 years	85-145 beats per minute
55 years	83-140 beats per minute
60 years	80-136 beats per minute
65 years	78-132 beats per minute
70 years	75-128 beats per minute

Note: The figures above are averages, so use them as general guidelines.

The three fundamental questions are:

Am I Hungry?
Is it Smart?
How Much Do I Need?

When you follow the Take 3 Method, you will learn how to enjoy foods, eat healthy, and achieve your weight loss goals.

Women's Daily Calorie Burn Table			
Current Weight	Non-Active (Most of the day sitting, driving a car, etc.)	Light (less than 2 hours of exercise per week)	Moderate (more than 2 hours of exercise per week)
110	1452	1573	1694
120	1584	1716	1848
130	1716	1859	2002
140	1848	2002	2156
150	1980	2145	2310
160	2112	2288	2464
170	2244	2431	2618
180	2376	2574	2772
190	2508	2717	2926
200	2640	2860	3080
210	2772	3003	3234
220	2904	3146	3388
230	3036	3289	3542
240	3168	3432	3696
250+	3300	3575	3580

Men's Daily Calorie Burn Table			
Current Weight	Non-Active (Most of the day sitting, driving a car, etc.)	Light (Less than 2 hours of exercise)	Moderate (more than 2 hours of exercise
110	1507	1628	1749
120	1644	1776	1908
130	1781	1924	2067
140	1918	2072	2226
150	2055	2220	2385
160	2192	2368	2544
170	2329	2516	2703
180	2466	2664	2862
190	2603	2812	3021
200	2740	2960	3180
210	2877	3108	3339
220	3014	3014	3498
230	3151	3151	3657
240	3288	3288	3816
250+	3425	3425	3975

WAPSE

For many years, while this author worked for the State of Wisconsin, she was a member of Wisconsin Association of Public Sector Employees. The members left work and traveled to conferences at one of the sponsoring hotels: Lake Geneva, Paper Valley, Oconomowoc over a weekend, once a year, for a three-day conference. Lake Geneva was bigger and became the choice hotel for the events.

Starting on Friday nights, the members left work and joined together for meetings scheduled. There were lots of workshops to attend. On Saturday morning some members would meet early to participate in a fun/run/walk for two to five miles. We danced with the group to get them started. We practiced dancing for a while before taking off. I used a boombox and selected music to keep their blood flowing, and stretching to avoid cramps in the legs. Some would walk or run to win a first place, last place, or the oldest in the group. After that, we separated to attend specific sessions. Most of the meetings were in different locations within the hotels. Sometimes we would have three meetings a day while attending the conference.

On Friday night, we had to check in at the hotel. On Sunday morning, we had church service and checked out, had breakfast, went back to a closing board meeting and traveled back home. We also had a yearly visit from former government representatives to comment on our dedication, and also gave a speech to encourage the employees.

On Saturday morning, we attended lectures. Most of the talks were focused on how to move up within the state system. On Saturday night, we dressed up for dinner, and afterwards changed again to dance to the music. There were coaches from personnel, Human Resources and an array of topics selected by the board of directors.

One of the times, about nine women went to one of the hotels for dinner and they had to wait an hour before a waitress came to serve the women. They were upset because everybody else were served except those nine women, although it looked like a big group. Finally, they got served, and did not want to leave a tip for the waitress, but left a penny as a tip because of poor service.

CAM

This author was a member of the Caribbean Association of Madison. For many years, I was dancing with CAM Dance Troupe. We practiced mostly at the Neighborhood House by University

Avenue. We used various costumes with white shirts and plaid skirts to dance the Limbo and Soca dance lyrics. The members were all from an African Caribbean descent namely Jamaica, British Guiana, Trinidad and Tobago, St. Lucia, Barbados, Virgin Islands.

We danced at Warner Park on the far north side of Madison. We used Calypso music or anything with good rhythm. Day of the event, CAM would always put us last to perform on stage, as everyone liked the way we moved and the beat from our music. We also encouraged visitors to join us on stage. In CAM, I was a treasurer for two years. I collected membership dues and provided a report for the board. I wrote checks for incurred expenses, reserved parks for the yearly picnics, reimbursed members for incurred expenses.

We gave out scholarships to High School students. When CAM became an organization with 501C3 status, we were able to do fundraisers. The scholarships were given to students with good grades and remarkable behaviors. The policy was for students who enrolled in some college to attain the scholarships. I wrote letters to the winners and issued certificates for a job well done.

MOTHER'S GRIEF

My mother lost her husband after he ate something that ceased his blood, which caused his death at the age of 35. We don't know if that was an allergic reaction, or a poison reaction from a snake bite. We do not have a record of what he ate.

Mother planted gardens and often hired people to weed and remove unwanted plants to help her garden grow its roots from separate parts, but thieves constantly stole from her. Once plants are established, the green or woody part of the plant can grow directly from the fibrous roots below, or often, the plant stem can produce new roots. Root tubers found in some plants can develop buds that will produce new plants. Once they uproot the plants, new buds are not generated anymore. We noticed footprints and discarded top branches from the plants. We knew there was a family that lived below a valley that stole other people's belongings, but never saw them in action. After the thieves were caught, the stealing stopped and everyone in the neighborhood were elated.

Mom planted bananas in one area and the bananas were always stolen. Sometimes she would be going to the garden which was located close to a river and she would hear someone running, but she could not see the individual which was in big daylight.

Mom had a place with lots of sheep and goats but the animals kept on disappearing. This was horrible as we often killed one of the animals for meat during the holidays, and we really did not have enough to purchase meat.

Etienne, my deceased brother planted lots of plants and seeds and found the crops were missing.

My sister caught people cutting wood to make boards from our property. She called the authorities, but the people returned the boards to her and were not arrested.

Sometimes mom would have to either tied her pigs or goats right under her house for fear of the thieves. During Christmas season, mom tied some of the animals in a room in the same house we slept. We could not keep a dog outside because the dog would bark and eventually disappear. These thieves were stealing both gardens and animals. My step-father had a similar problem with thieves stealing from his gardens. His house was on top of a hill facing these people.

MEDICAL TERMS
AND DEFINITIONS

Blood Pressure: -Although it causes no symptoms, high blood pressure could boost the risks of leading killers such as heart disease, stroke, aneurysm, cognitive decline, and even kidney failure.

Cardiovascular: - Medical circulatory system, which comprises the heart and blood vessels and carries nutrients and oxygen to the tissues of the body and removes carbon dioxide.

Cholesterol: -Understand what your cholesterol levels should be: Total, **LDL, HDL, Triglycerides, VLDL**, the normal range with a chart to easily interpret any lipid test.

Circulation: -Orderly movement through a circuit; especially the movement of blood through the vessels of the body 2. Flow, 3. Passage or transmission from person to person or place to place; especially the interchange of currency.

Chronic Disease: A disease that persists for a long time. A chronic disease is one lasting 3 months or more, by the definition of the U.S. National Center for Health.

Diabetes mellitus type 2.: (Also known as Type 2 Diabetes) is a long-term metabolic disorder that is characterized by high blood sugar, insulin resistance, and relative lack of insulin. Common symptoms include increased thirst, frequent urination, and unexplained weight loss. Risk factors.

Disease: - A disease is a particular abnormal condition that negatively affects the structure or function of part or all of an organism, and that is not due to any external injury. Diseases are often construed as medical conditions that are associated with specific symptoms and signs. A disease may be caused by external factors such as pathogens or by internal dysfunctions. For example, internal dysfunctions of the immune system can produce a variety of different diseases, including various forms of immunodeficiency, hypersensitivity, allergies and autoimmune disorders.

Genetics: - The science of heredity, dealing with resemblances and differences of related organisms resulting from the interaction of their genes.

Healthiness: - The condition of being sound in body, mind, or spirit; especially freedom from physical disease or pain. How to use health in a sentence.

Heart Disease: - In general, chest pain, or angina, is a common symptom of heart disease. You may feel discomfort in your chest. Some people experience tightness or a squeezing sensation around their breastbone. The pain may radiate to the neck, down the arms.

Legumes: - The most common varieties of legumes are beans. These include adzuki bens, black beans, soybeans, fava beans, garbanzo beans, (chickpeas), kidney beans, and lima beans. These foods are high in protein and carbohydrates but low in fat.

Majority: - The majority is the greater part, or more than half, of the total. It is a subset of a set consisting of more than half of the set's elements. "Majority" can be used to specify the voting requirement, as in a "majority vote". A majority vote is more than half of the votes.

Muscles: - Orderly movement through a circuit; especially: the movement of blood through the vessels of the body induced by the pumping action of the heart. 2: flow. 3a: passage or transmission from person to person or place to place; especially the interchange of currency.

Overall Health: - An individual's "Overall Health" from the perspective of Health Economics is composed of three parts. Understanding Overall Health will assist you with evaluating the changes in your clients from before to after an accident. The first part is called "the self-perceived, or self-rated health".

Overweight: - Weight that is higher than what is considered as a healthy weight for a given height is described as overweight or obese. Body Mass Index, or BMI, is used as a screening tool for overweight or obesity. Adult Body.

Peptic Ulcer: - Poor sleep quality and peptic ulcer disease (PUD, a condition when sores known as ulcers develop on the lining of your stomach or in the first part of your small intestine) are both major public health problems that affect the physical and psychological wellbeing of older adults.

Seizure: - Medical condition sudden, uncontrolled electrical disturbance in the brain which can cause changes in behavior, movements, feelings, and consciousness.

Stroke – The amount of blood pumped by the left ventricle of the heart in one contraction. The stroke volume is not all the blood contained in the left ventricle, normally, only about two-thirds of the blood in the ventricle is expelled with each beat.

Wellness: - the state of being in good health, especially as an actively pursued goal.

Whole Grains: - A whole grain, also called a wholegrain, is a grain of any cereal and pseudo-cereal that contains the endosperm, germ, and bran, in contrast to refined grains, which retain only the endosperm. As part of a general healthy diet, consumption of whole grains is associated with lower risk of several diseases. Whole grains are a source of carbohydrates, multiple nutrients and dietary fiber. Cereals proteins have low quality, due to deficiencies in essential amino acids, mainly lysine.

ACKNOWLEDGMENT
AND APPRECIATION

Steps to Reverse Diabetes

This book has a lot of dedicated professionals – all the writers I started to read, <u>Media Ripe vs. Green Bananas Which are better for you?</u> All the teachers I have learned from, all the students, all the editors, all the colleagues, all the friends, all the family. And speaking of family, let me start with special thanks to my mom, Rita, my dad Gerald, and siblings, Robert, Jerome, Etienne, Reginald, uncle Feddy, who have passed away. Very special thanks to my sister Helena, Valerie, Valendice, Aaron, my husband Joseph, Lina, Elaine, Geannette, Doni, and Darian, for providing their encouragement in my writing, and pursuing my dream, and in memory of my brothers and mother mentioned above who have passed away.

Thanks to my writing teachers Mrs. Watts, for what I know today and learned from her at the El Paso Community College in

Business Report Writing class, Kenley's College in St. Lucia, and the Madison Area Technical College for learning Fundamentals of Speech Writing. Thanks to my nutritionists from UW Health and doctors at UW Hospital. Thanks to Jennifer and Alex, Mia for being good neighbors. Thanks to Harry, Denis, Lina, Elaine and some of my fans at St. Maria Goretti Church, Linda, Kaari, Margaret, Sue, Marla, Mike, Bill, Tam for purchasing my cookbooks.

Perseverance helps us to live our faith when it is difficult. We do not give up even when it is not easy to do something good.

Thanks be to God and praise to you Lord Jesus Christ. God the father, son and the holy spirit, we give you thanks and praise, Amen.

Lifeline Nutrition solutions nutritionists for providing me with subscription for nutrition and Type 2 Diabetes articles. Thanks to Consumer Report on Health which brings health secrets yet so effective on health and wellness. Thanks to the Meadowridge Library for their assistance.

My husband, Joseph Herman, provided technical support. He also gave terrific neck rubs and shoulder massages, and laughed with me over the funny parts.

Thanks to Madison Area Technical College teacher and students for sharing their ideas and opened my eyes in putting this memoir together.

Thanks to Authorhouse Solutions for providing webinars, podcast, Memoir Writing by its Author Support in Indiana.

Thanks to Fr. Scott Emerson Parochial Administrator of St. Maria Goretti Church for his faith and guidance in writing this book. His advice to have a prayer printed in this book is appreciated.

ACKNOWLEDGMENT
AND APPRECIATION

Author:	Anne Marie Herman, Retired State and University Worker
Style and Format	Aaron Herman, Provided Business Cards Information
Proof Reader Assistant	Barb Booth, Made Suggestions
Proofing & Assembling	Joseph Herman, Made Suggestions
Consultant	Valerie Payne, Provided Opinion on Structure

Whether you are creating a memoir or a personal essay, writing about your own life can be a daunting task: How much do you remember? What's important to include in your story? What about truth and artistic license? How do you even get started mining a life's worth of memory?

From drawing a map of a remembered neighborhood to writing from old notebooks, brochures, to composing open letters that reveal the power of your own voice, author Anne Marie Herman, who has written Anne Marie's Family Favorite Recipes with a Caribbean Twist, offers innovative techniques that will trigger ideas for all writers of creative nonfiction.

Lightning Source UK Ltd.
Milton Keynes UK
UKHW012344190220
359015UK00002B/8/J